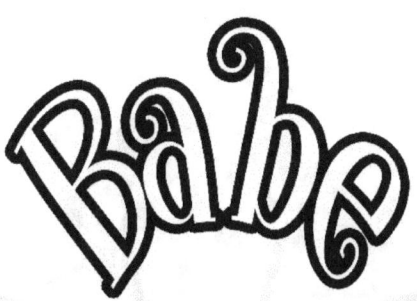

Babe

Valentine's Day Coloring Book

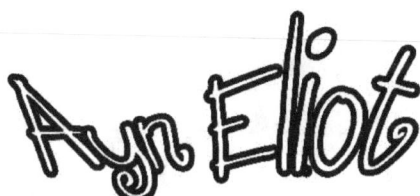

Ayn Eliot

Happy Coloring

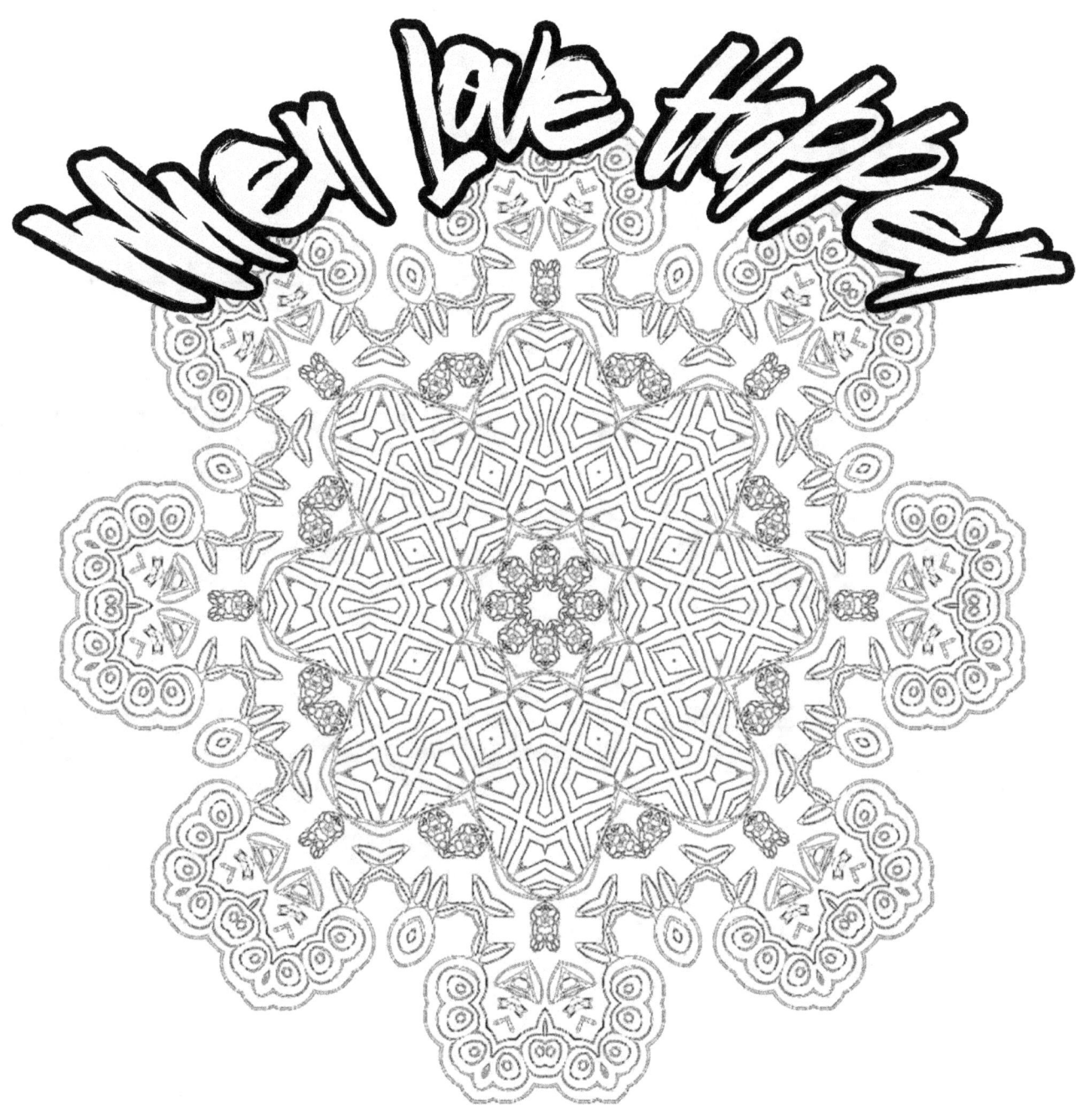

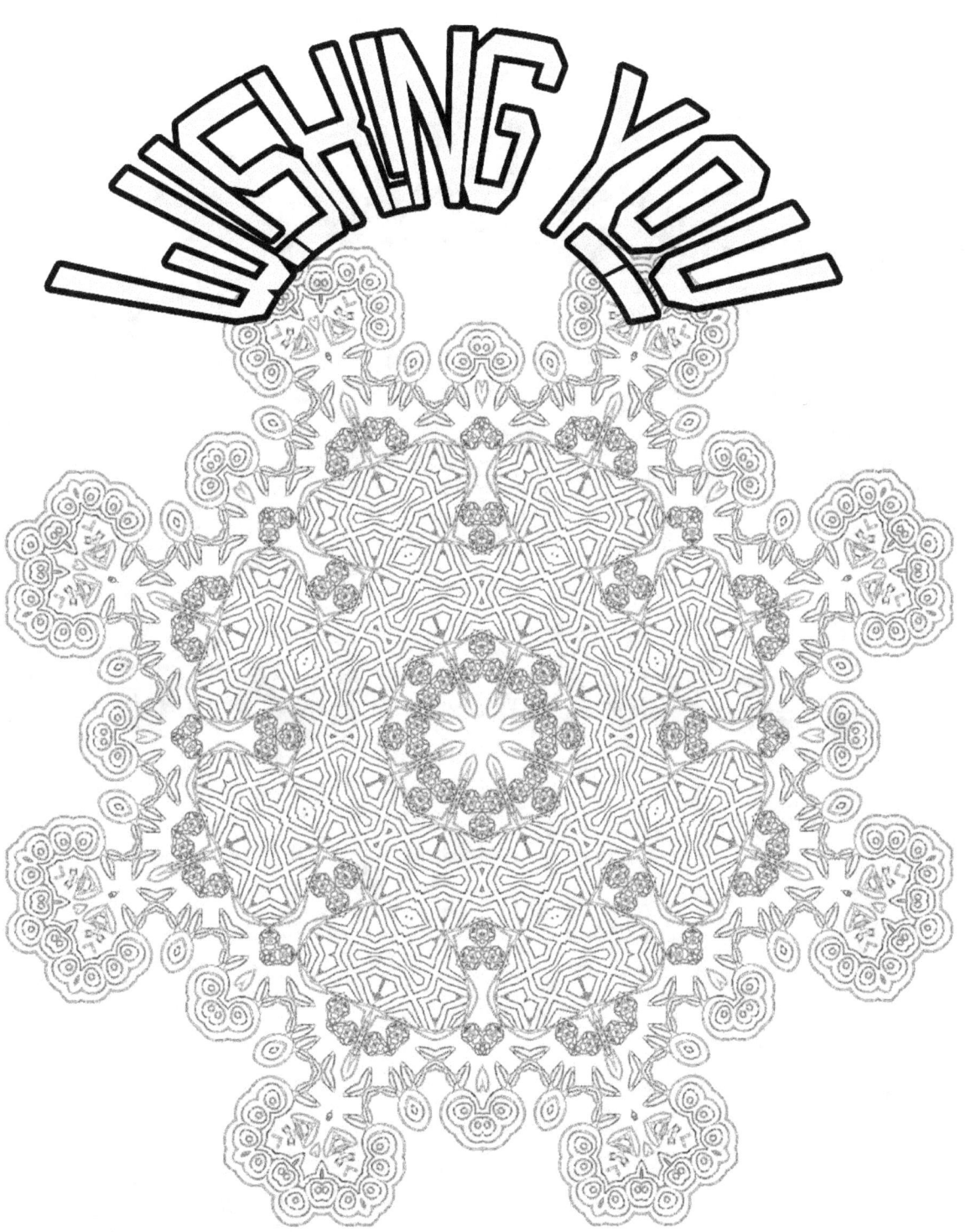

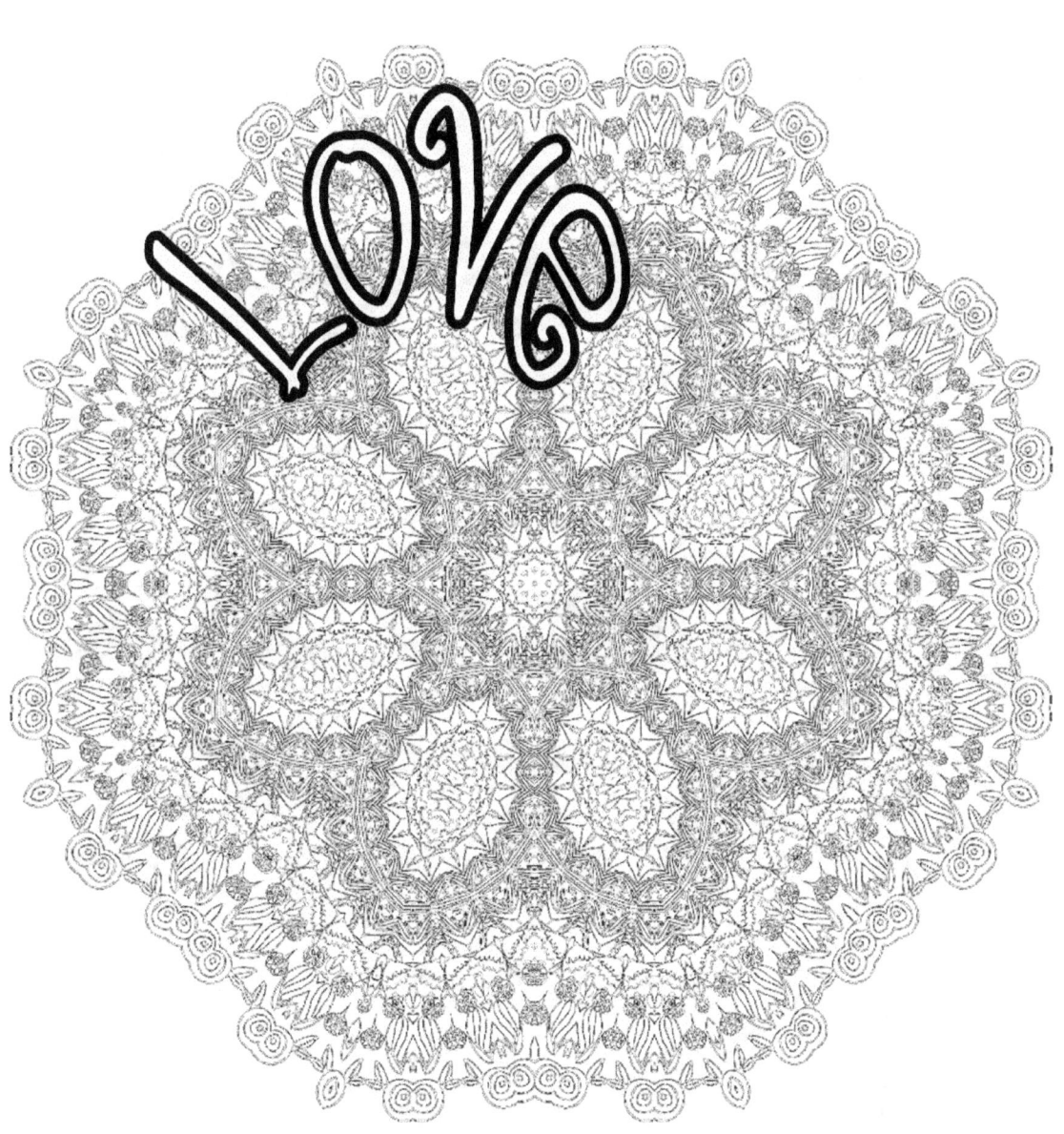

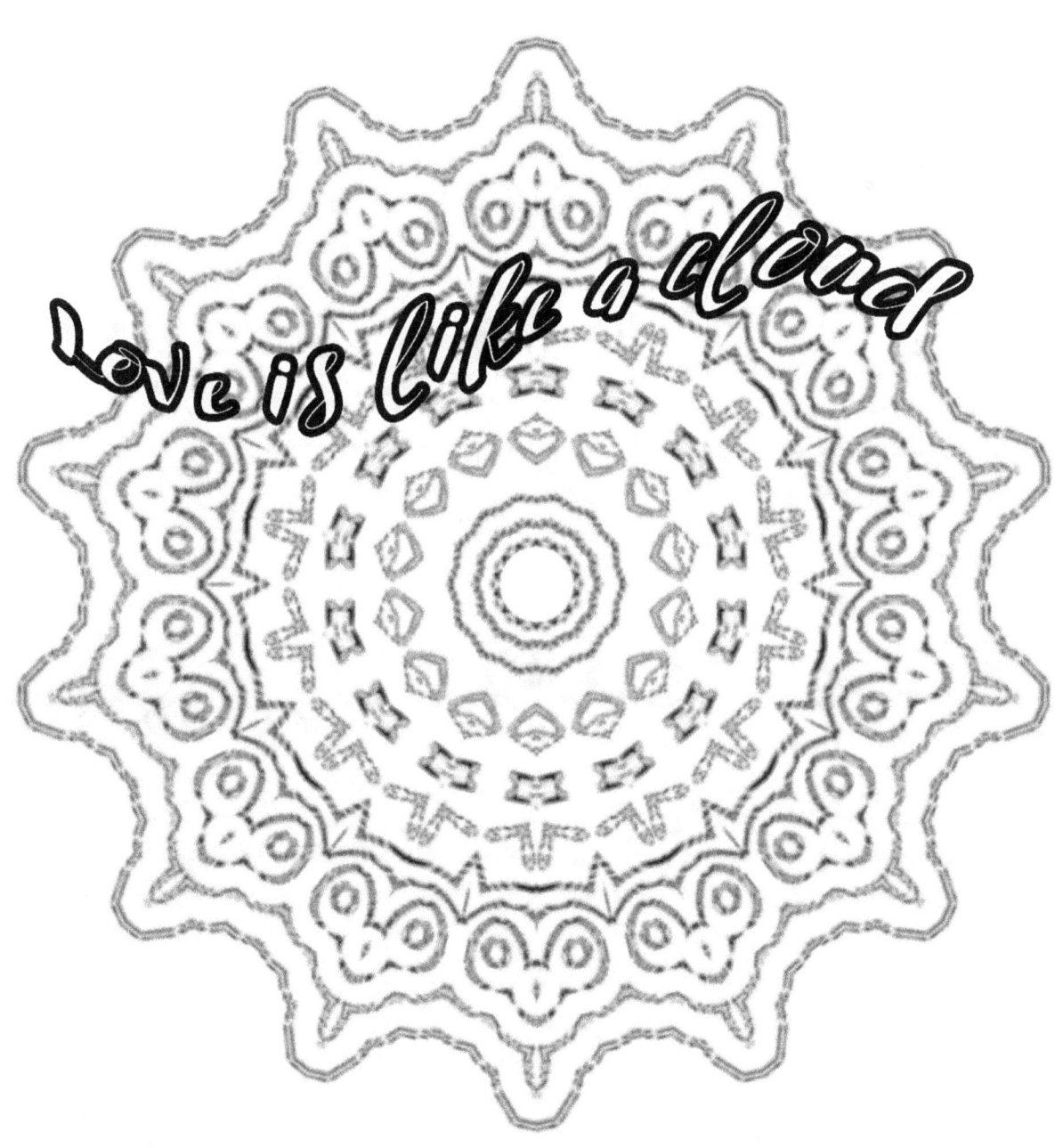

love is like a cloud

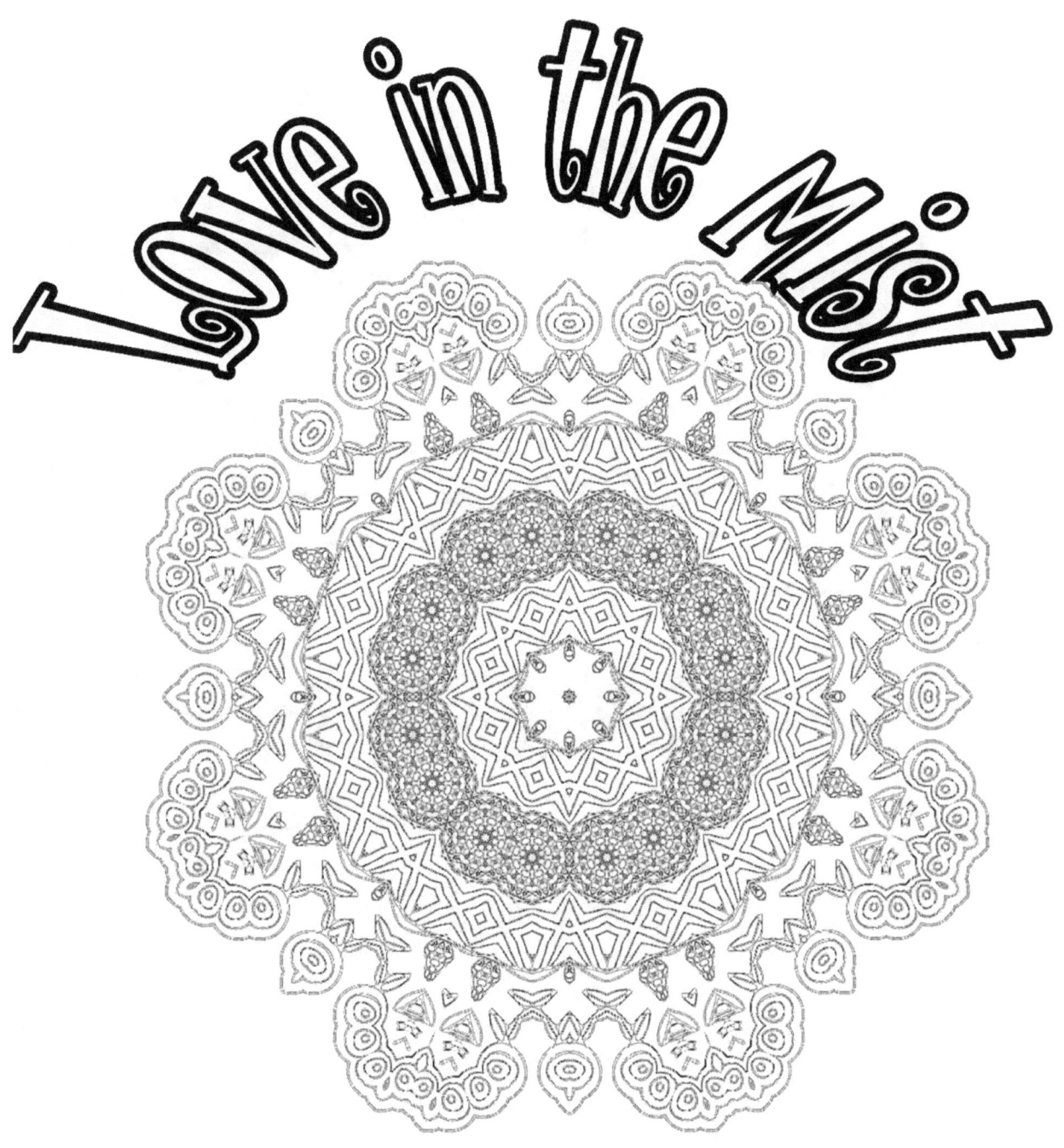

Love in the Mist

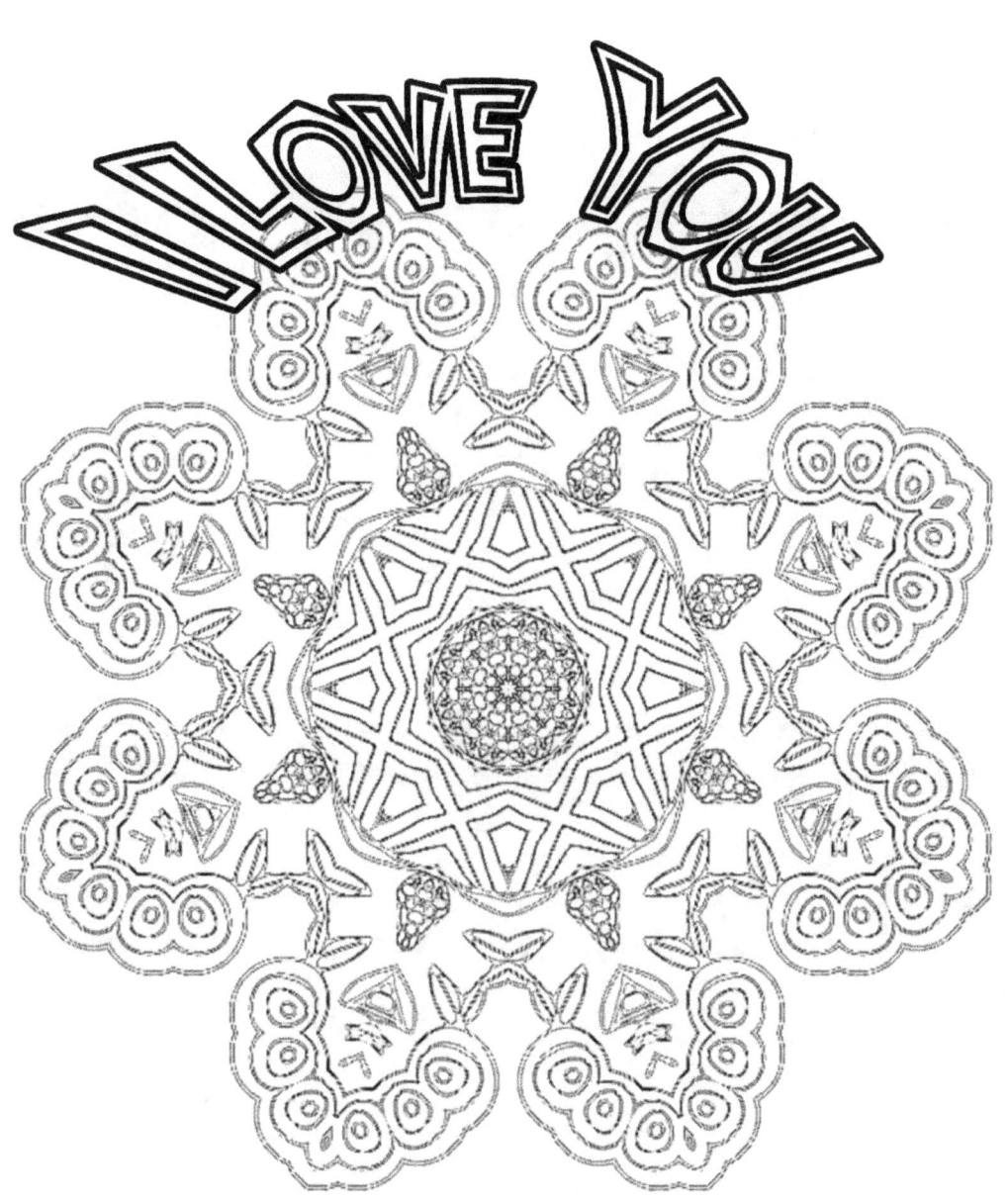

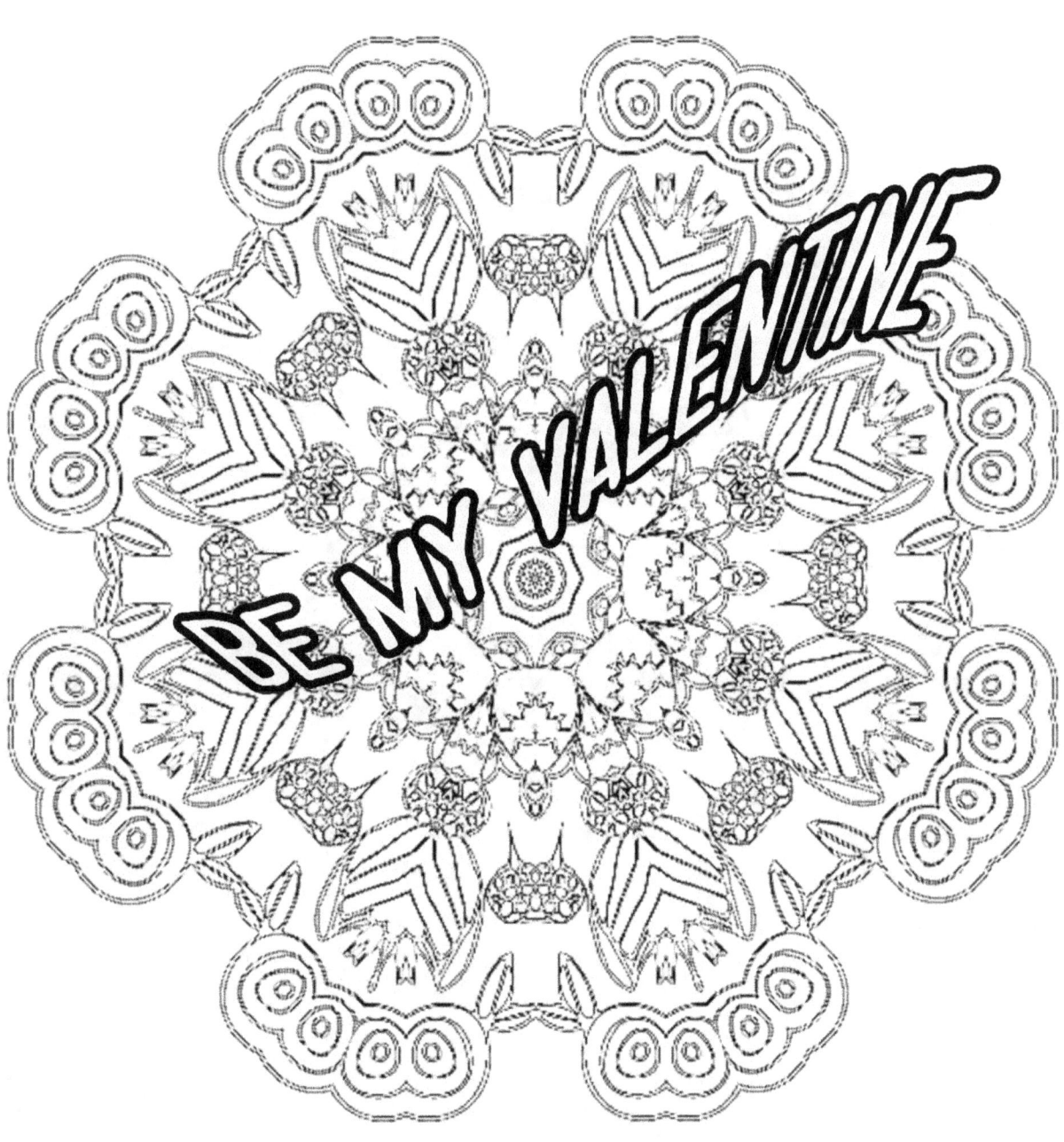

Love at the first site

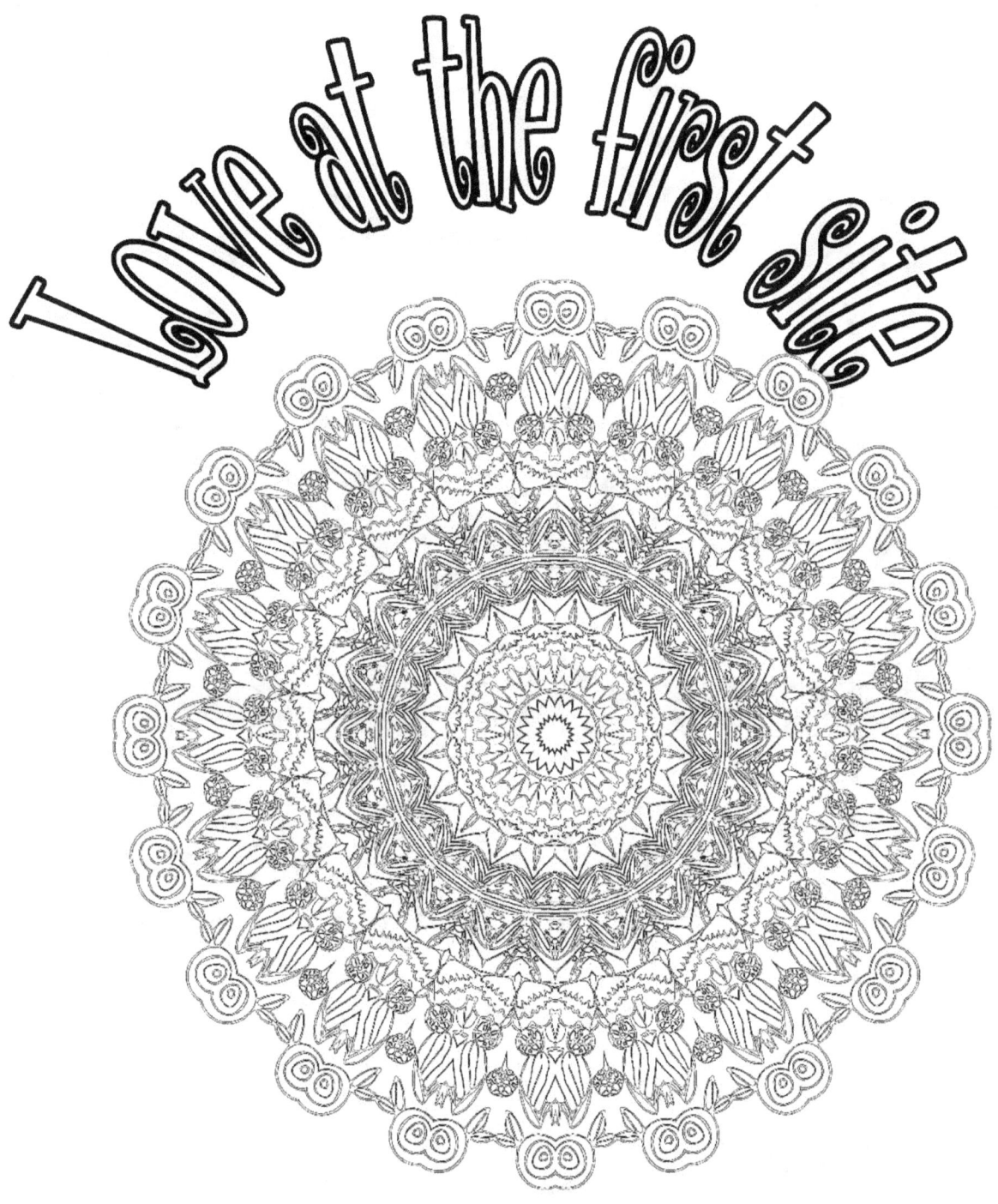

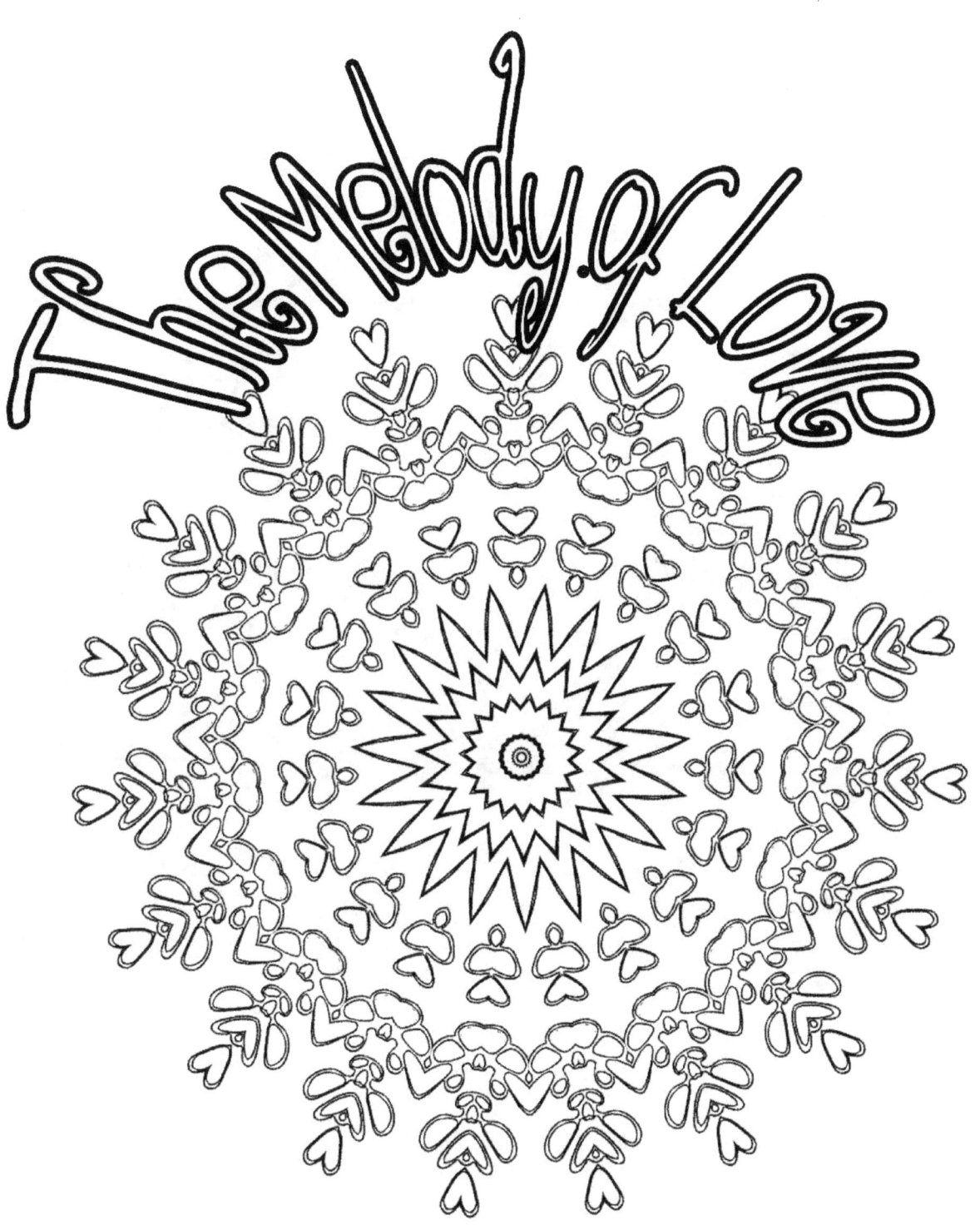

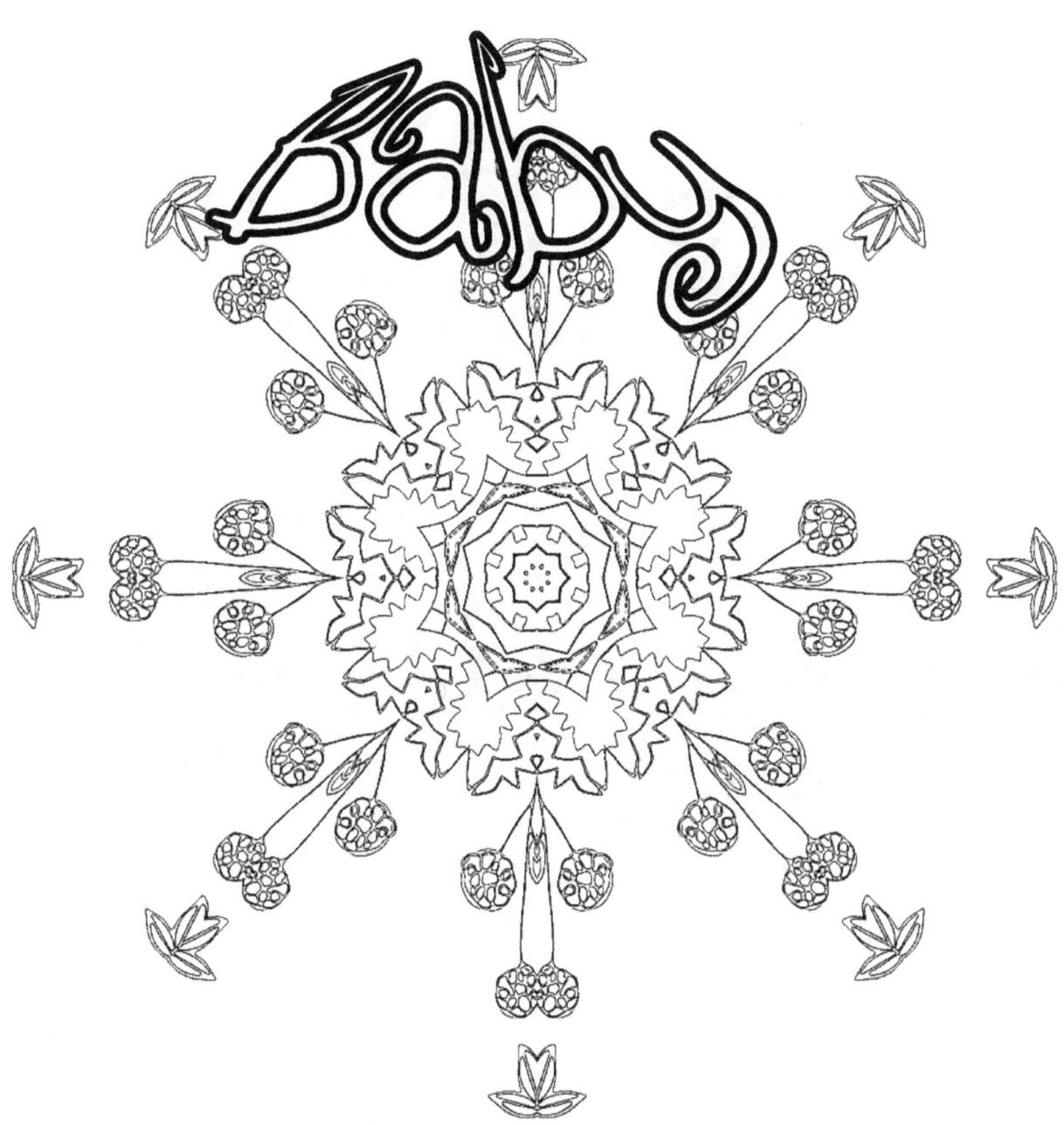

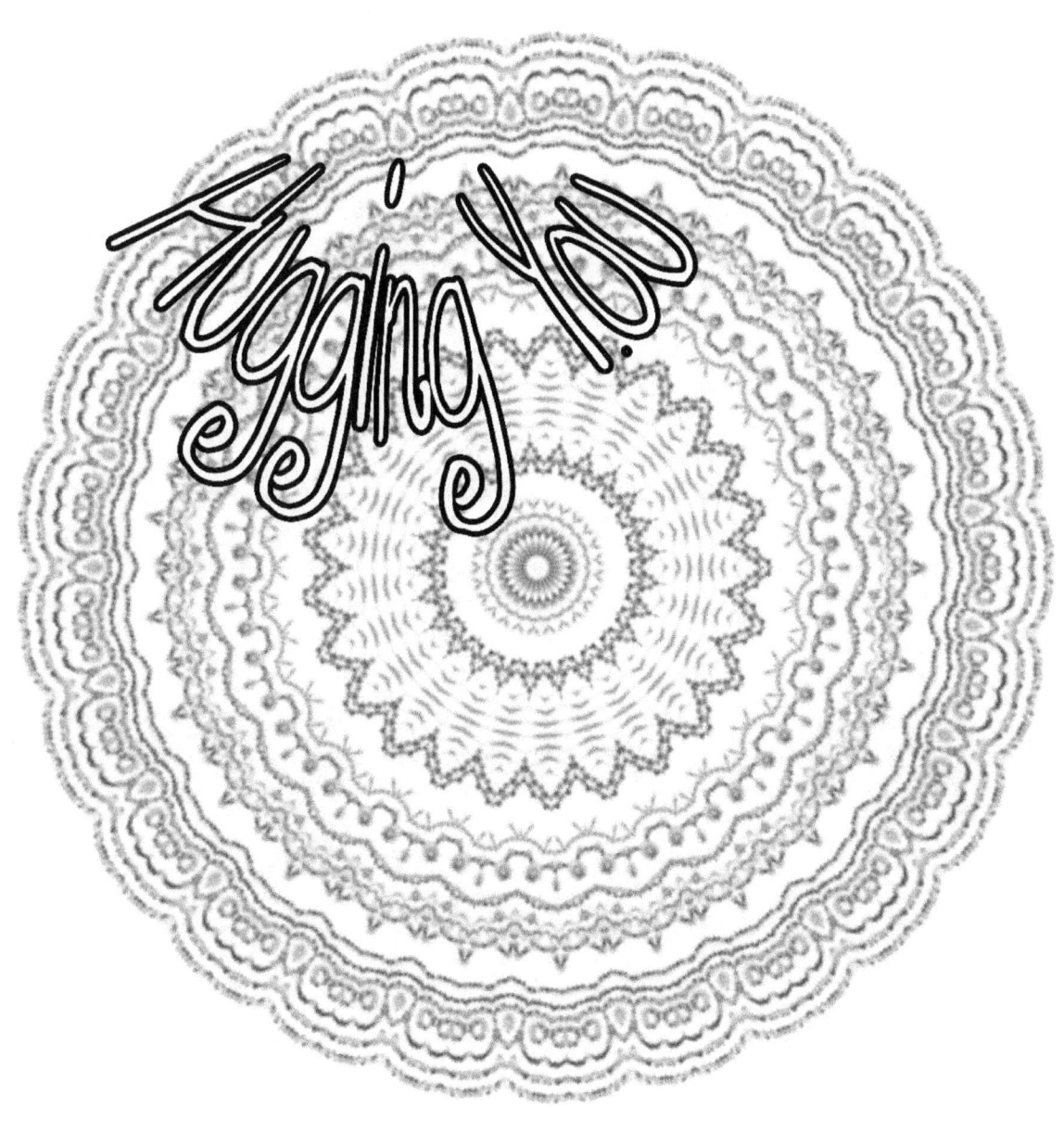

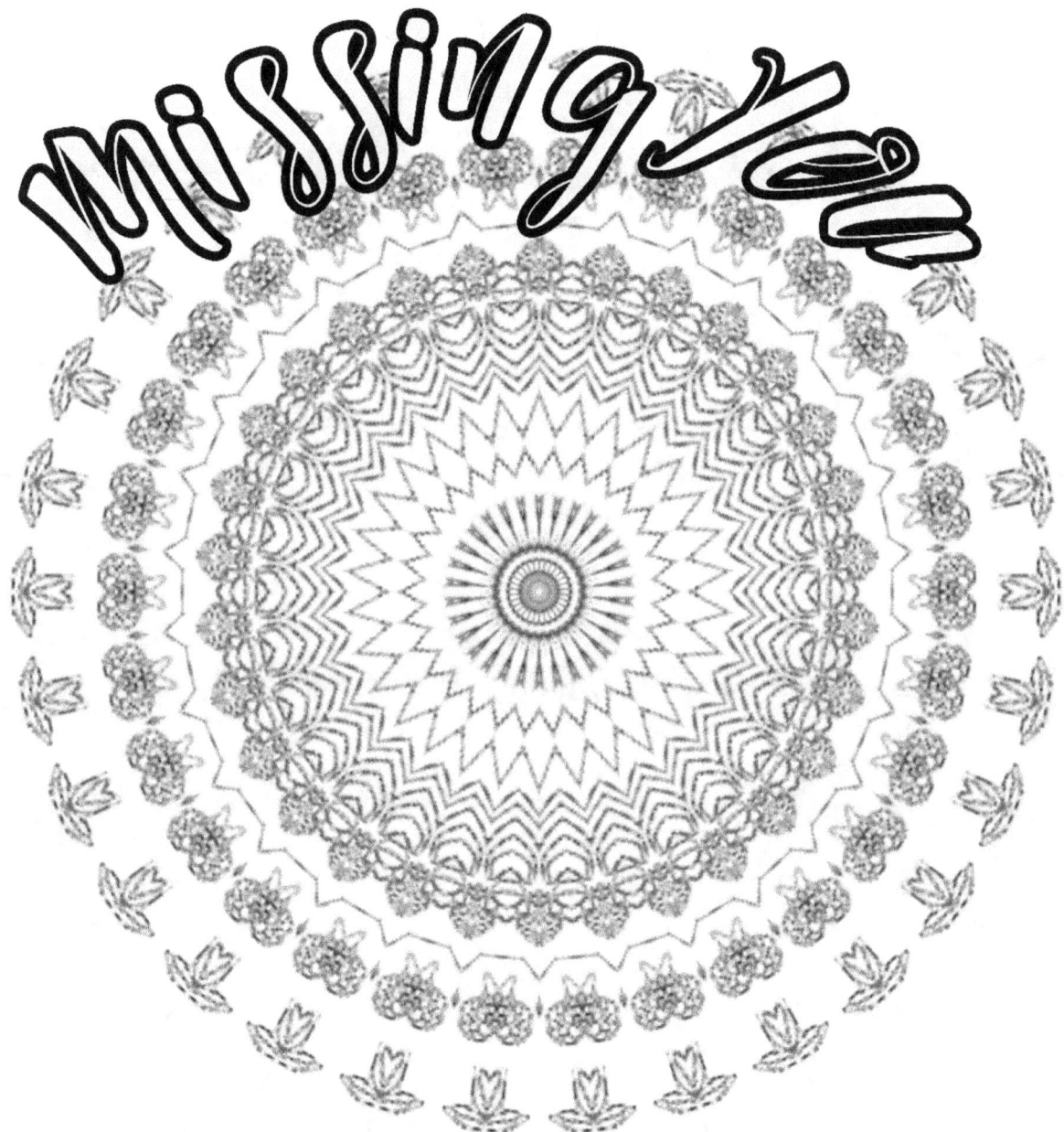

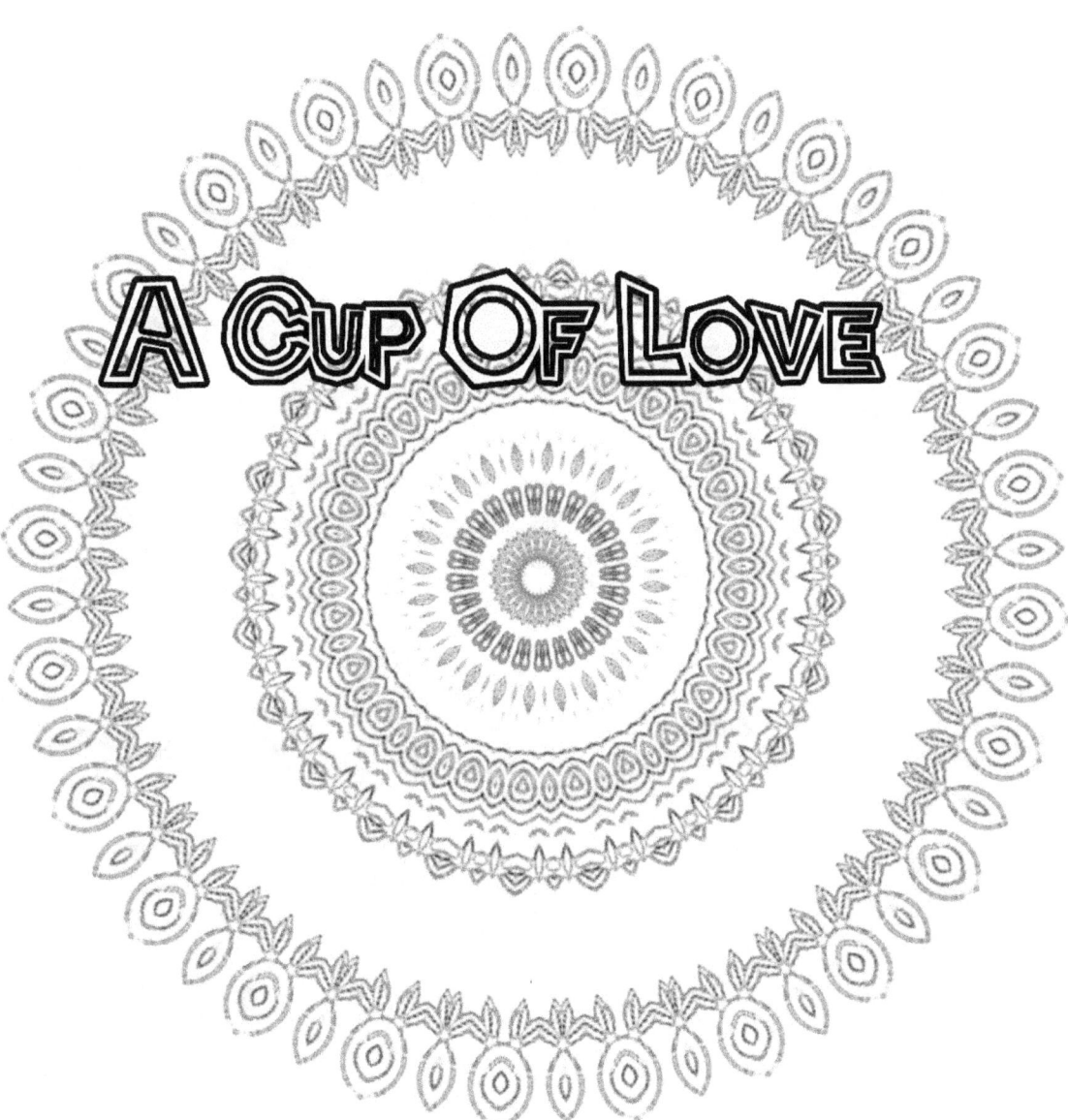

A Cup Of Love

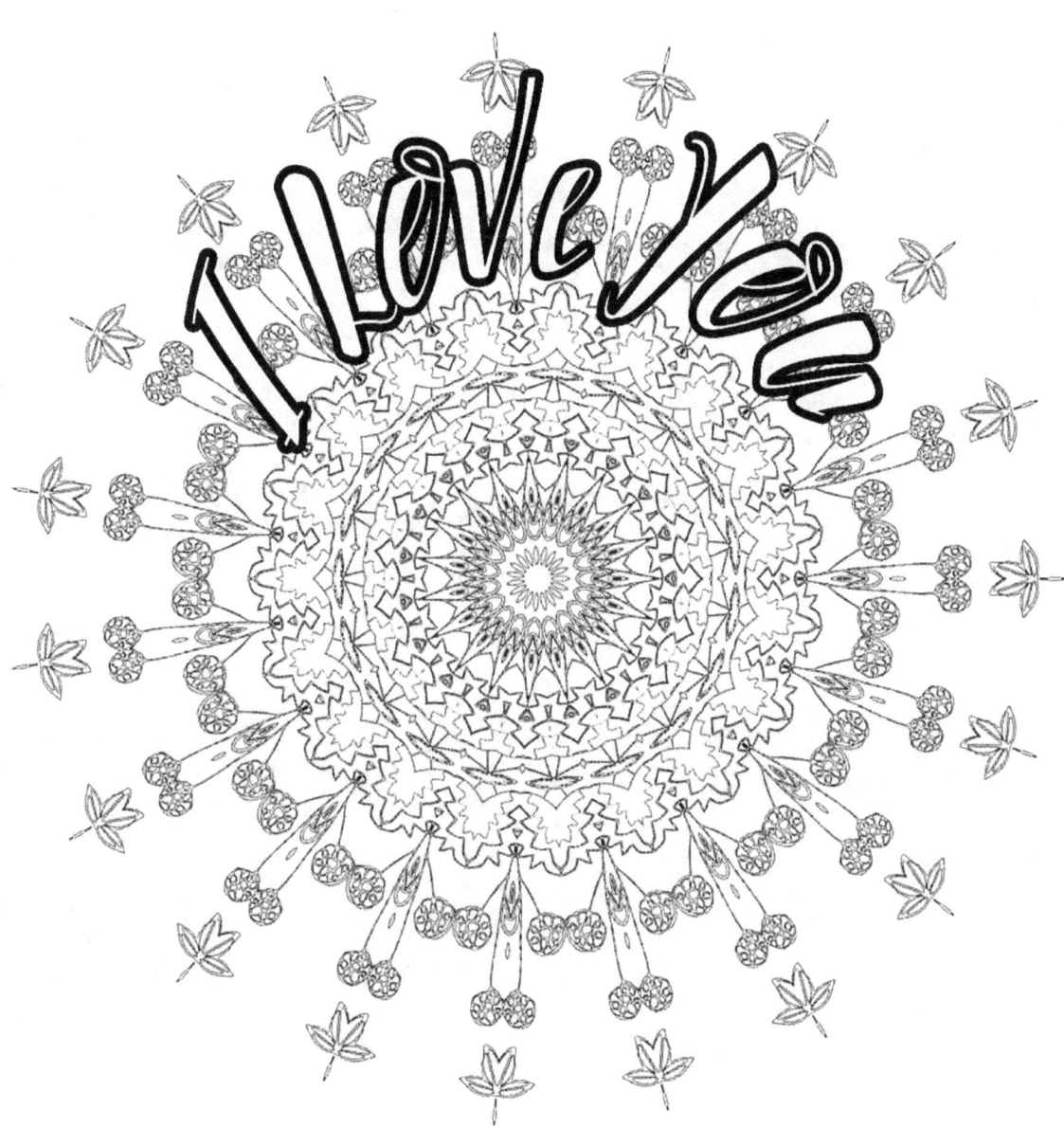

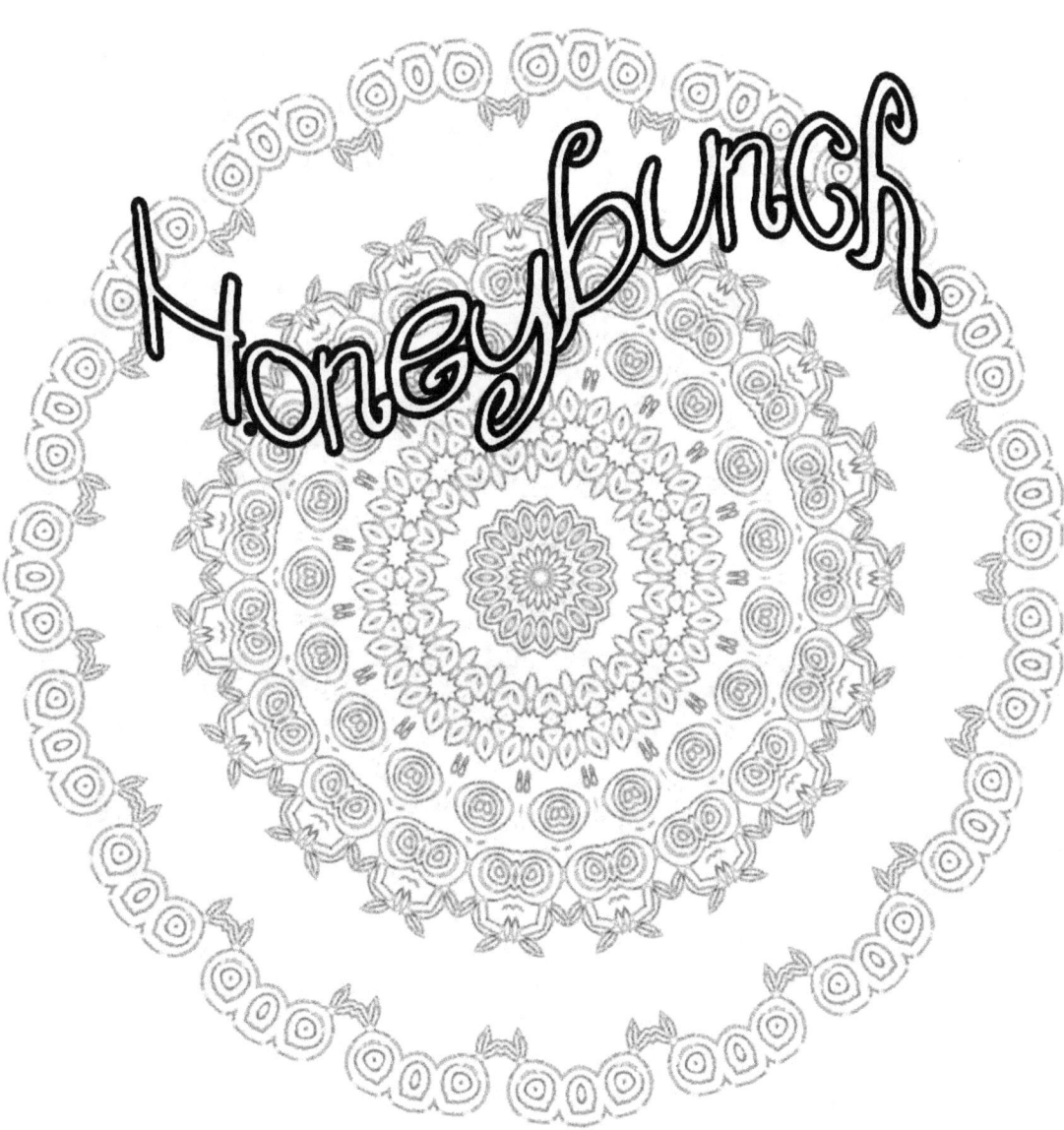

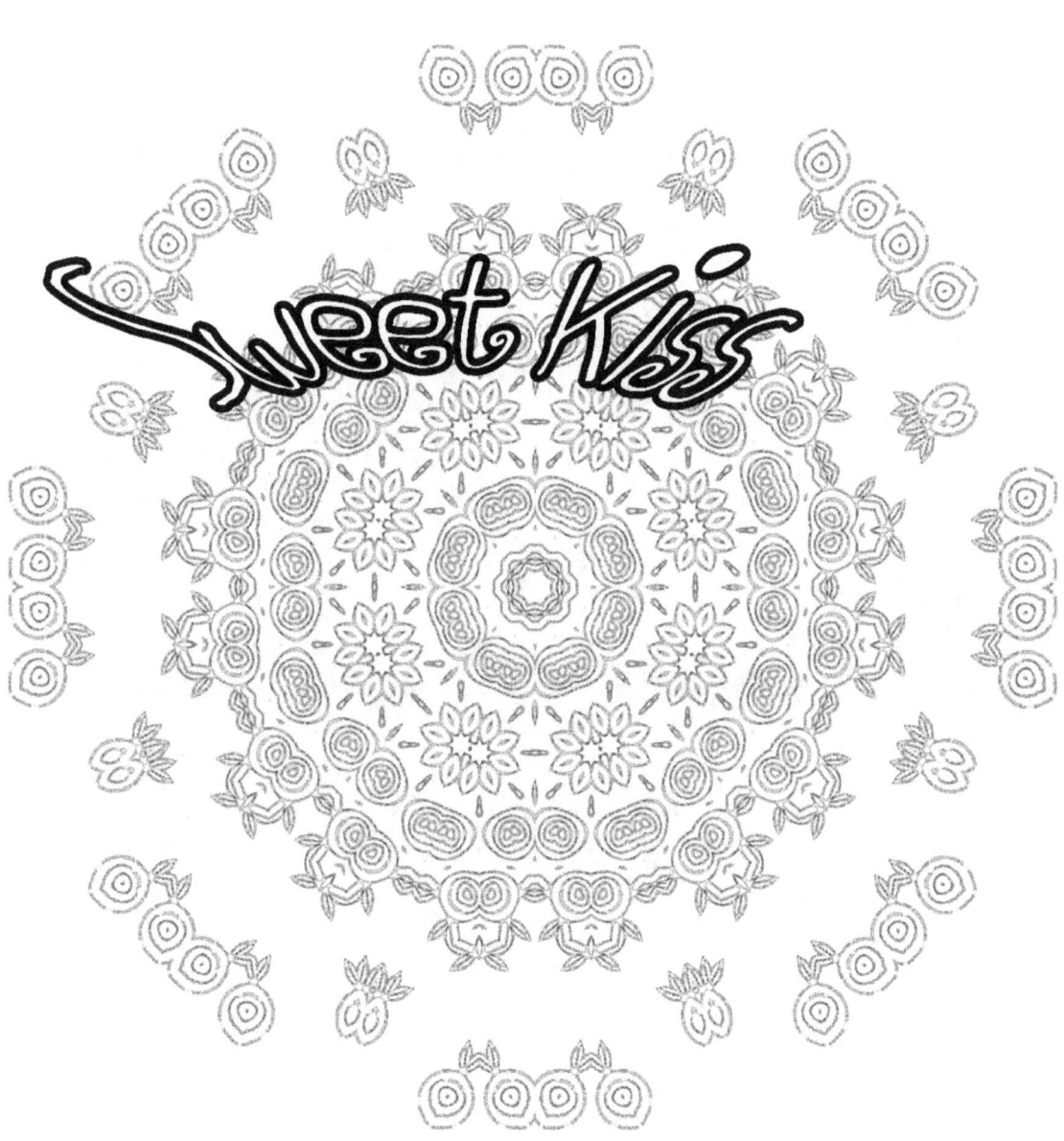

love is like a dream

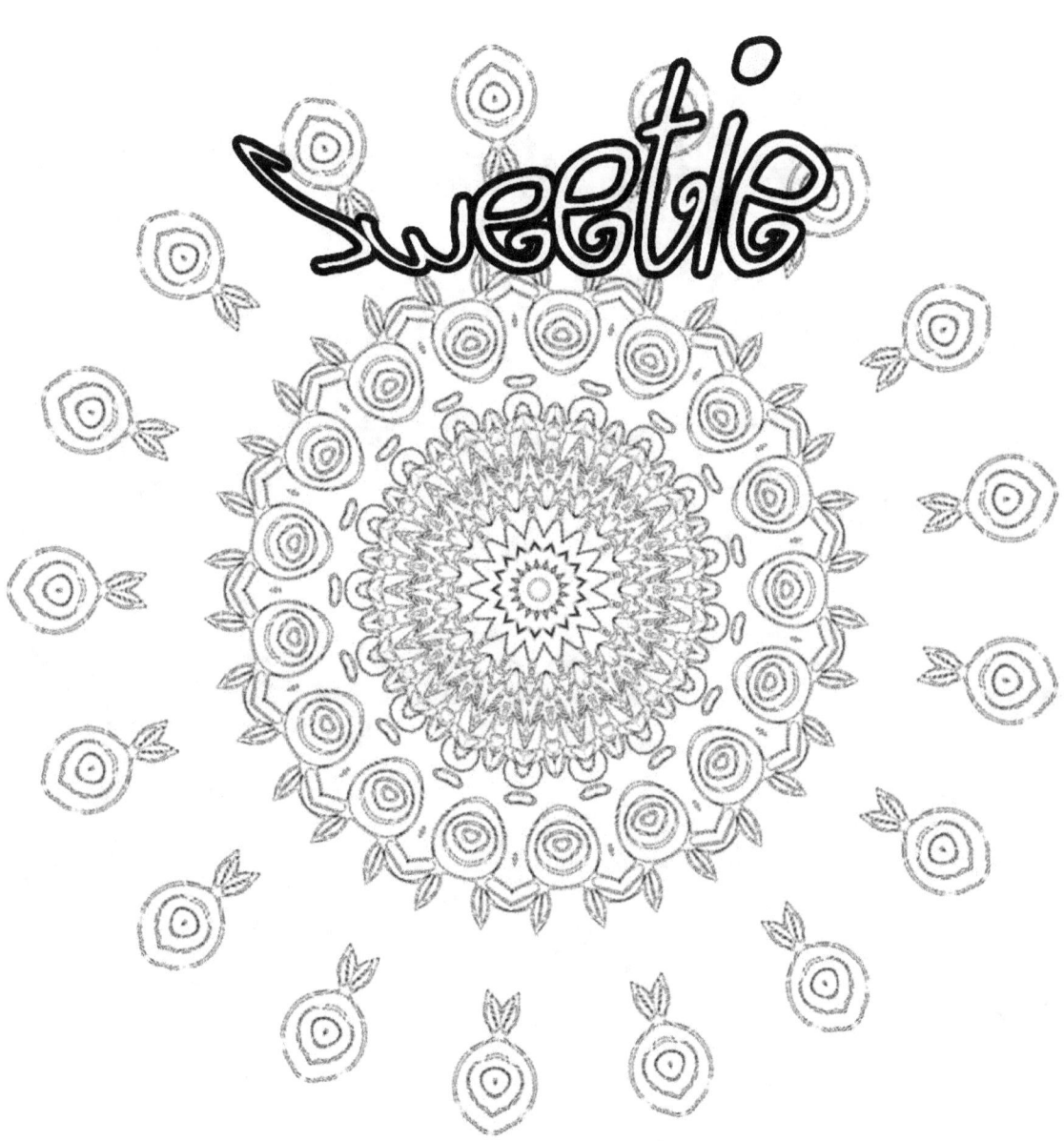

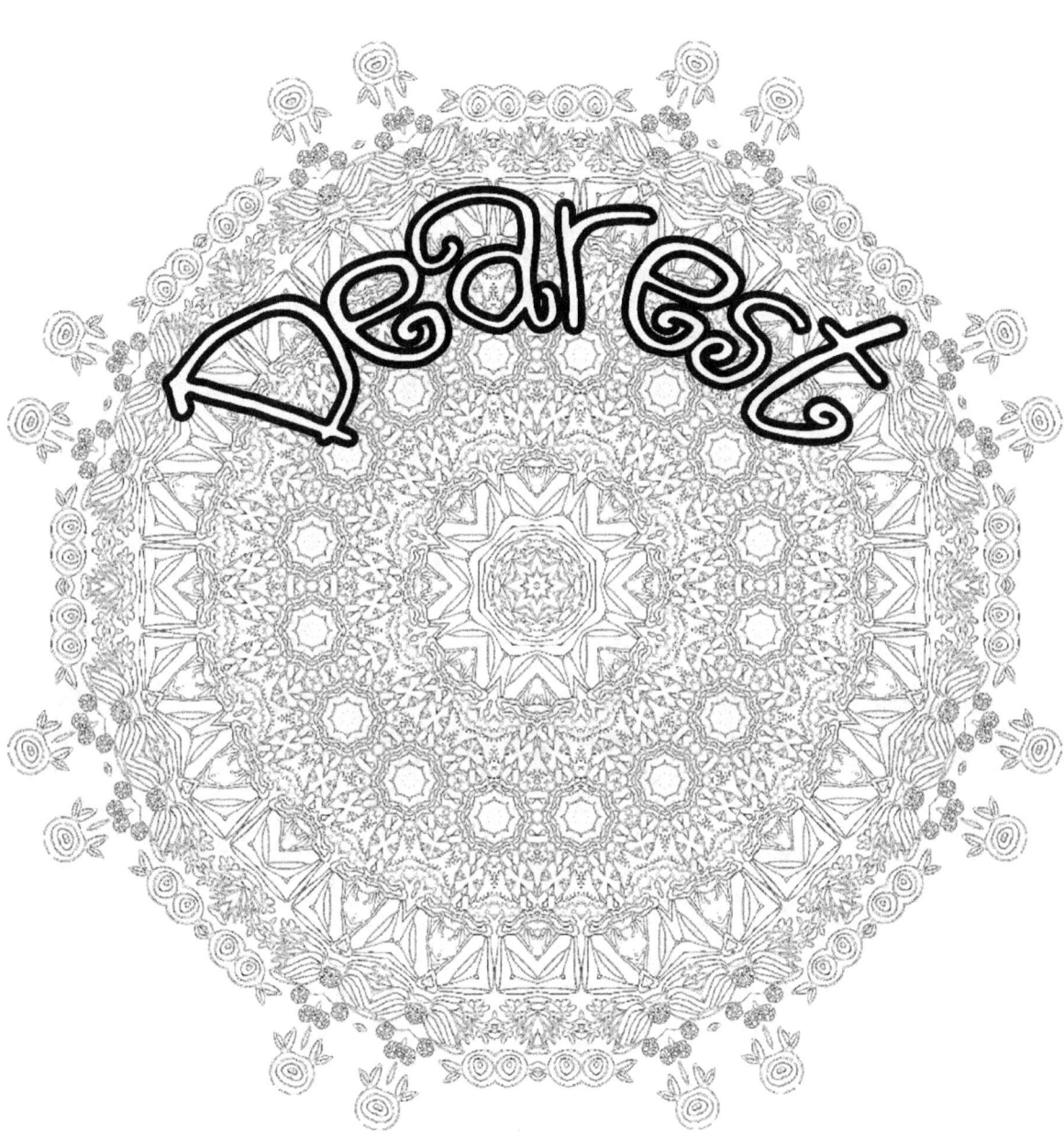

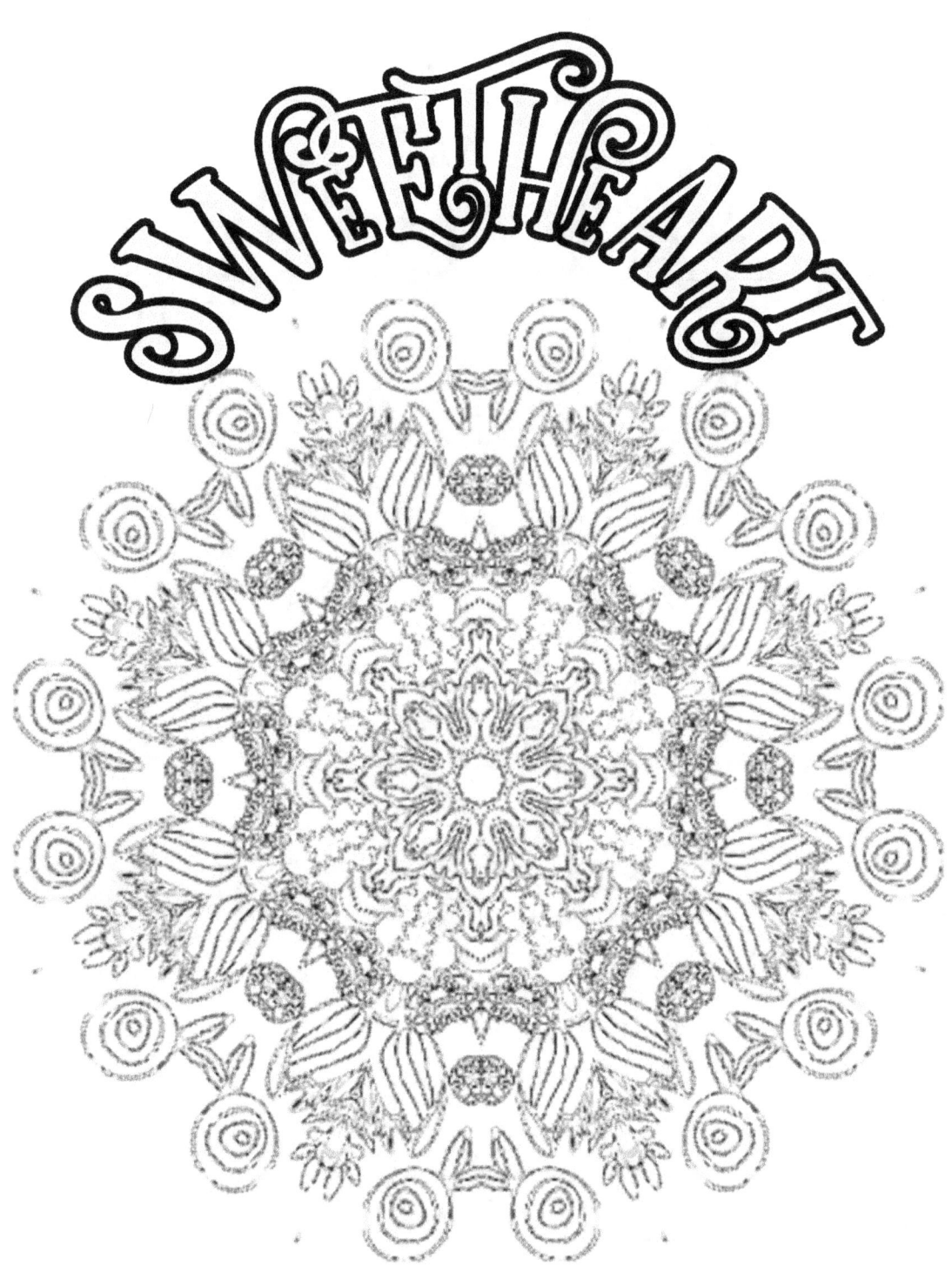

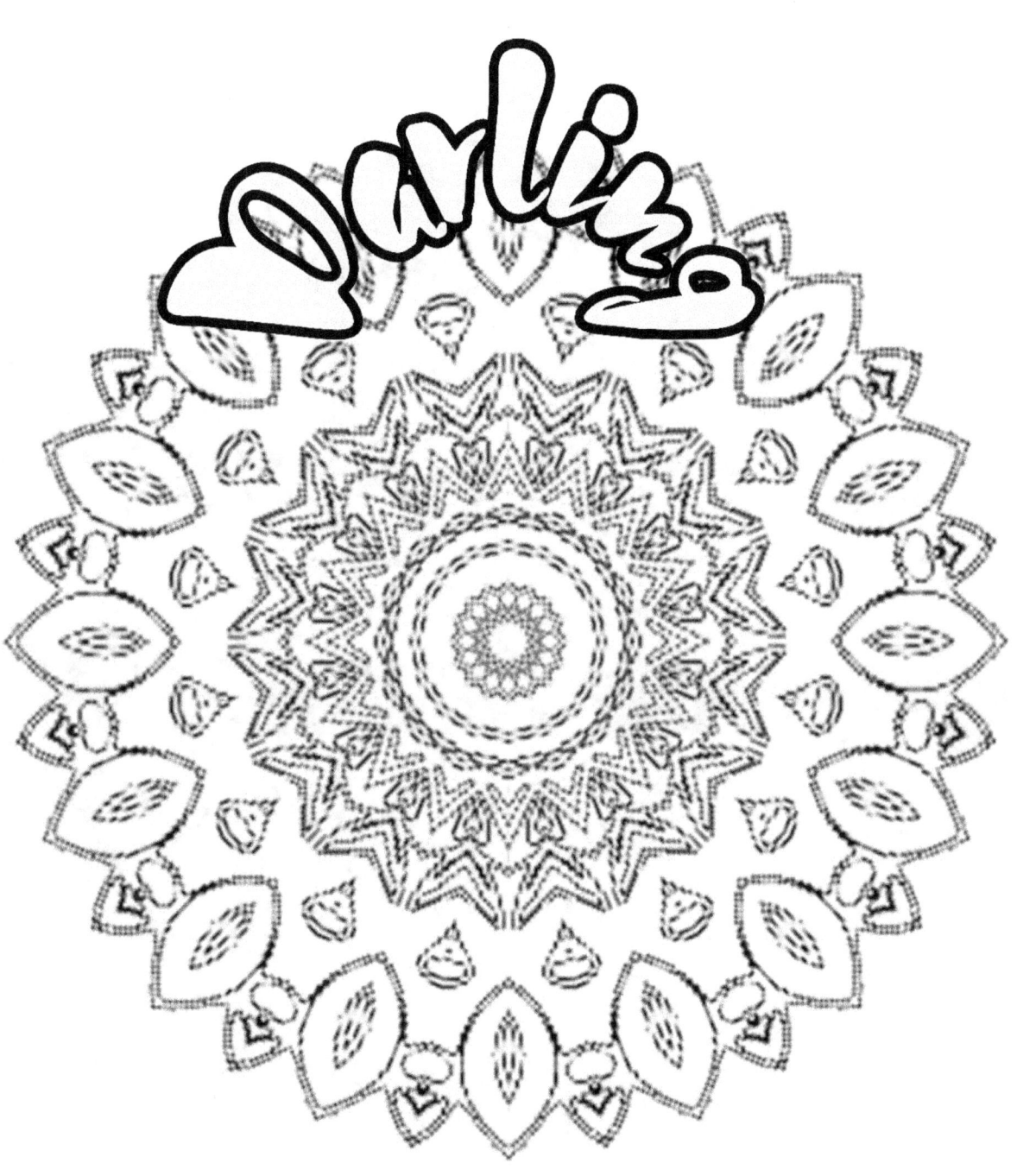

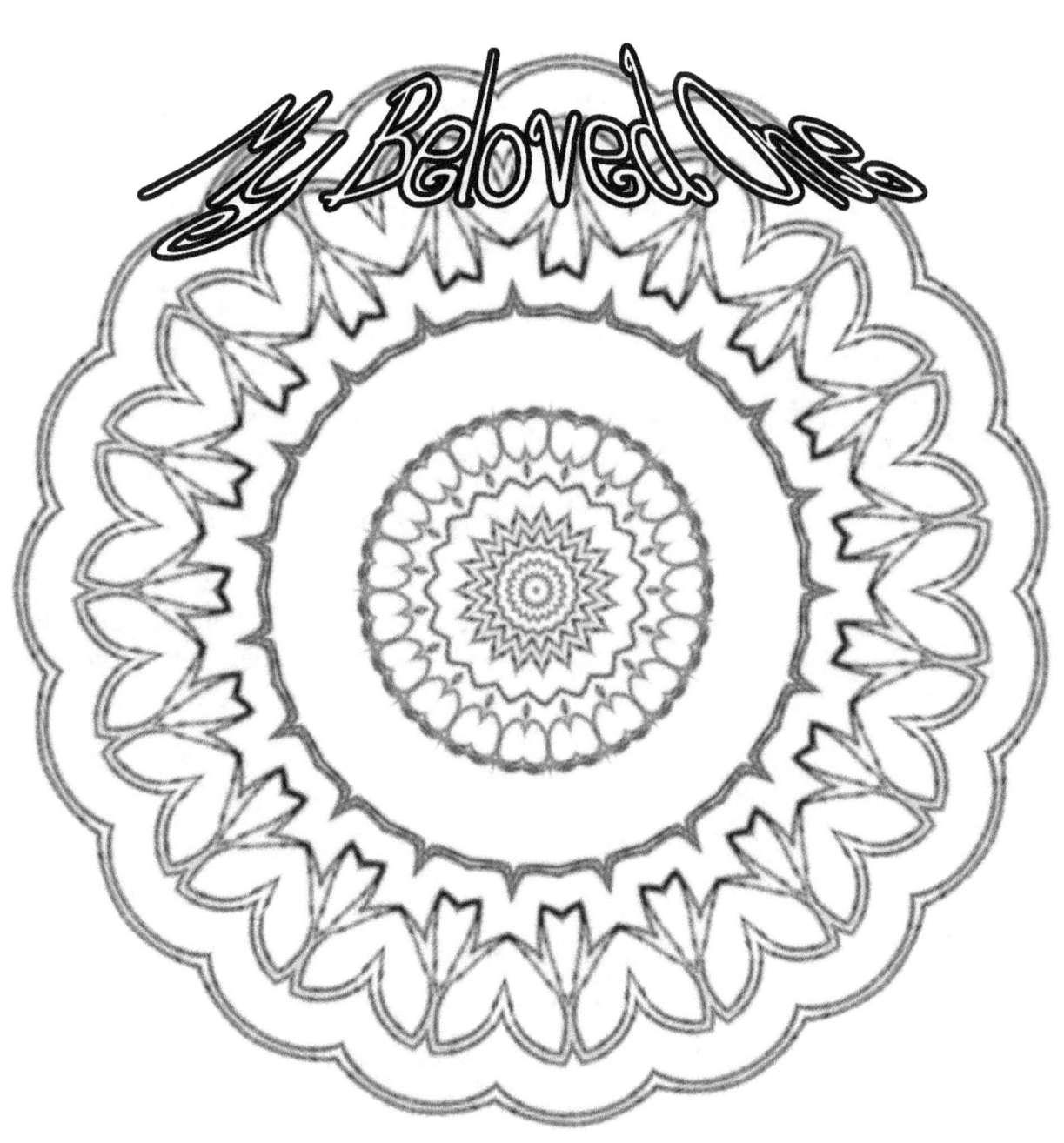

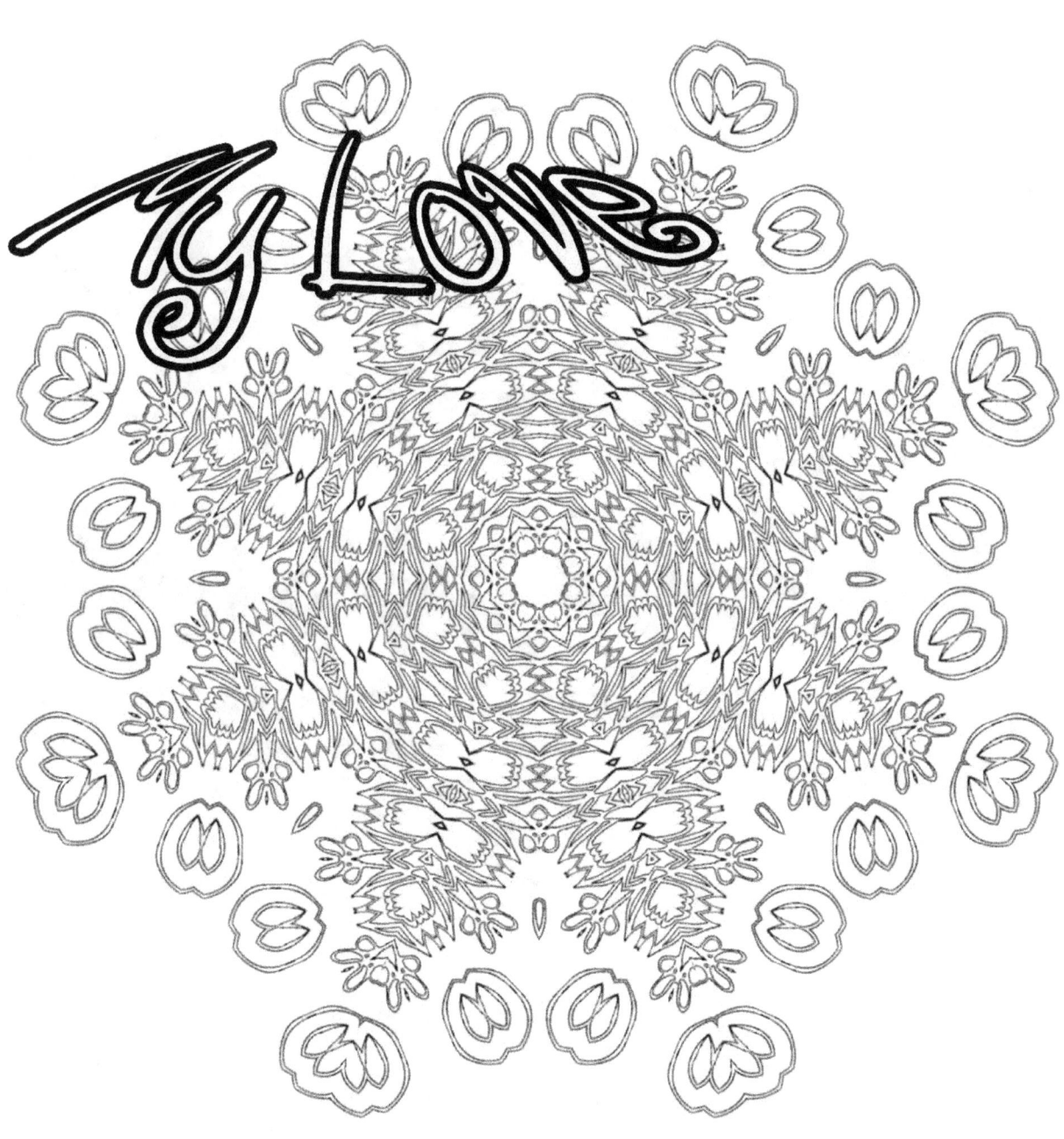

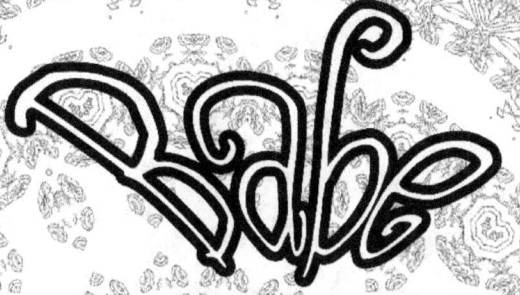

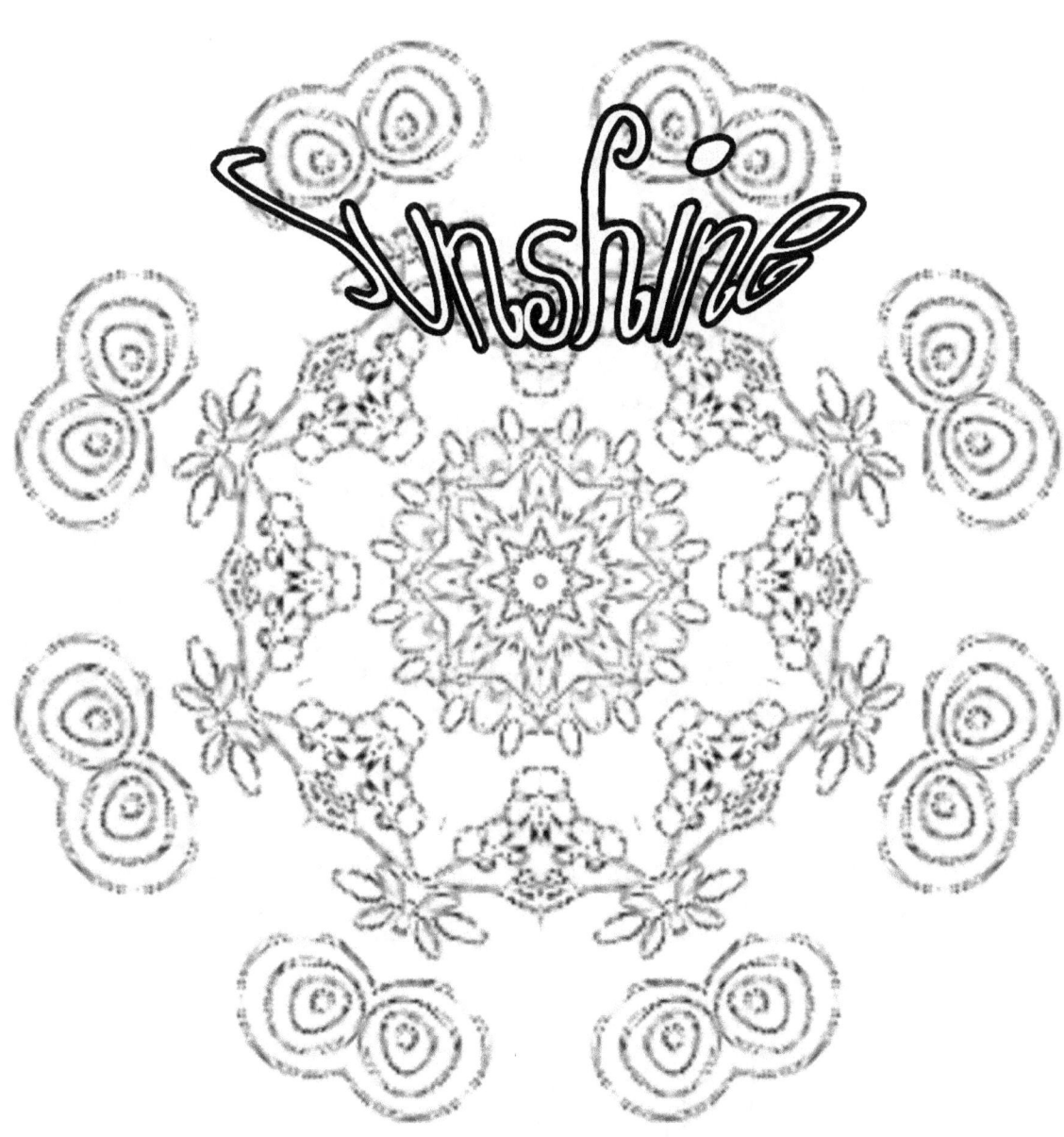

www.ingramcontent.com/pod-product-compliance
Lightning Source LLC
Chambersburg PA
CBHW081747170526

45167CB00009B/3958